Looking at Countries

IRELAND

Kathleen Pohl

W
FRANKLIN WATTS
LONDON•SYDNEY

This edition first published in 2008 by Franklin Watts

Franklin Watts
338 Euston Road
London NW1 3BH

First published in 2008 by Gareth Stevens Publishing
1 Reader's Digest Road
Pleasantville
NY 10570-7000 USA

Dewey number: 914.17
ISBN: 978 0 7496 8245 3

Senior Managing Editor: Lisa M. Guidone
Senior Editor: Barbara Bakowski
Creative Director: Lisa Donovan
Designer: Tammy West
Photo Researcher: Sylvia Ohlrich

Photo credits: (t=top, b=bottom)
Cover (main) Will & Deni McIntyre/Corbis; Cover (inset) Gideon Mendel/Corbis; title page Peter Adams
Photography/Alamy; p. 4 Derek Croucher/Alamy; p. 6 Nagelestock.com/Alamy; p. 7t Michael Diggin/Alamy; p. 7b
scenicireland.com/Christopher Hill Photographic/Alamy; p. 8 Peter Titmuss/Alamy; p. 9t Nagelestock.com/Alamy; p. 9b
Daniel Barillot/Masterfile; p. 10 Isifa Image Service s.r.o./Alamy; p. 11t Marmaduke St. John/Alamy; p. 11b Christian
Kober/Alamy; p. 12t Bill Bachmann/Alamy; p. 12b Dennis Cox/Alamy; p. 13 Authors Image/Alamy; p. 14t Will & Deni
McIntyre/Corbis; p. 14b AA World Travel Library/Alamy; p. 15t David Lyons/Alamy; p. 15b Ingolf Pompe/Aurora
Photos; p. 16 Art Kowalsky/Alamy; p. 17t SC Photos/Alamy; p. 17b Liam White/Alamy; p. 18 Searagen/Alamy; p. 19t
Peter Adams Photography/Alamy; p. 19b Ros Drinkwater/Alamy; p. 20t Paul Lindsay/Alamy; p. 21 Foodfolio/Alamy; p.
22t Liam White/Alamy; p. 22b Gideon Mendel/Corbis; p. 23t Bill Bachmann/Alamy; p. 23b Marshall
Ikonography/Alamy; p. 24 Julian Herbert/Getty Images; p. 25t scenicireland.com/Christopher Hill Photographic/Alamy;
p. 25b Michael Diggin/Alamy; p. 26 Paul Thompson Images/Alamy; p. 27t Richard Naude/Alamy; p. 27b Javier
Larrea/SuperStock. Every attempt has been made to clear copyright. Should there be any inadvertent omission
please apply to the publisher for rectification.

Printed in China

Franklin Watts is a division of Hachette Children's Books, an Hachette Livre UK company.
www.hachettelivre.co.uk

Contents

Where is Ireland?   4

The landscape   6

Weather and seasons   8

Irish people   10

School and family   12

Country   14

City   16

Irish homes   18

Food   20

At work   22

Having fun   24

Ireland: the facts   26

Glossary   28

Find out more   29

Some Irish words   30

My map of Ireland   31

Index   32

Where is Ireland?

Ireland lies to the west of Great Britain in the Atlantic Ocean. It is an island and has one land border, with Northern Ireland. Northern Ireland takes up roughly one sixth of the island and is part of the United Kingdom.

Did you know?

All of Ireland was once ruled by Great Britain. In 1921 it won independence.

The Custom House in Dublin, Ireland's capital, houses government offices.

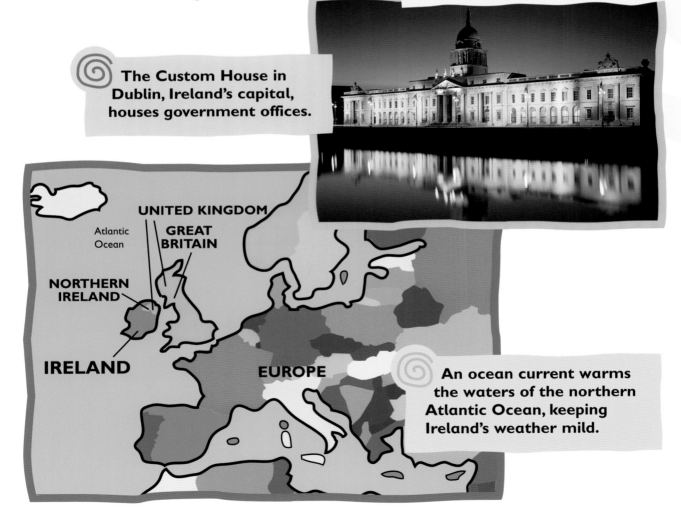

An ocean current warms the waters of the northern Atlantic Ocean, keeping Ireland's weather mild.

Atlantic Ocean

UNITED KINGDOM

GREAT BRITAIN

NORTHERN IRELAND

IRELAND

EUROPE

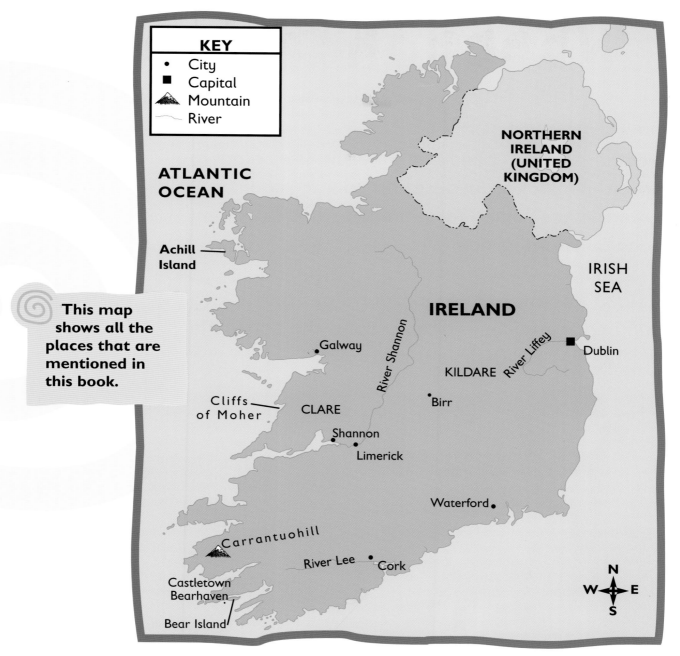

KEY
- • City
- ■ Capital
- 🏔 Mountain
- 〰 River

ATLANTIC OCEAN

NORTHERN IRELAND (UNITED KINGDOM)

Achill Island

IRISH SEA

This map shows all the places that are mentioned in this book.

IRELAND

Galway

River Shannon

River Liffey

■ Dublin

KILDARE

Cliffs of Moher

CLARE

• Birr

Shannon

Limerick

Waterford •

Carrantuohill

Castletown Bearhaven

River Lee

• Cork

Bear Island

N
W — E
S

On the east, the Irish Sea separates Ireland from the island of Great Britain. The Atlantic Ocean washes the south, west and north-west coasts.

Ireland's full name is the Republic of Ireland. It is divided into 26 counties. The capital city, Dublin, is the centre of government and business in Ireland.

The landscape

Ireland is often called 'the Emerald Isle', after the green gemstone, because the countryside is so green. It has rolling farmland, pastures, swampy peat bogs and green hills.

Ireland has several mountain ranges and a large number of smaller islands around the coast. Many are famous for their beauty.

Achill Island lies off the west coast of Ireland. Achill has high sea cliffs and sandy beaches. It also has farms and small villages.

The steep Cliffs of Moher are in County Clare in western Ireland.

Did you know?

Ireland has more than 12,000 lakes. They are fed by the country's high rainfall each year.

Ireland has many sandy beaches and rugged cliffs. Its longest river, the River Shannon, runs through the middle of the country.

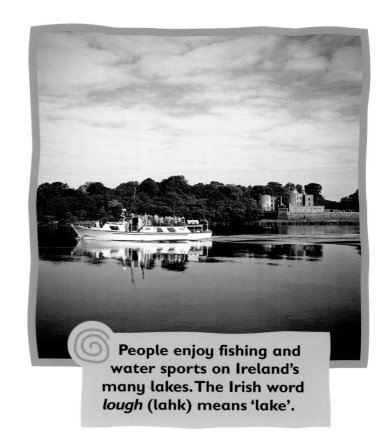

People enjoy fishing and water sports on Ireland's many lakes. The Irish word *lough* (lahk) means 'lake'.

Weather and seasons

Ocean breezes that blow across Ireland keep the weather mild and wet. Irish people often say their country has 40 shades of green. This is because plants grow well in wet weather.

In the low-lying areas of Ireland, about 90 centimetres of rain fall each year. Mountains and hills can get up to 250 centimetres of rainfall each year.

The sunniest and driest months are April, May and June. In those months, most parts of Ireland get about six hours of sunshine each day. December is the dullest month, with only about one hour of sunshine daily.

Did you know?

Rain in Ireland often falls as a fine mist. The Irish people call such days 'soft days'.

The Irish are used to wet weather.

A rainbow shines over the northwest coast of Ireland.

Plenty of rain keeps the Irish countryside green all year round.

Like the United Kingdom, Ireland has four different seasons but they are all mild. The average summer temperature is 15°C. In winter, the average temperature is 5°C. Compared with the coasts, inland areas are warmer in summer and colder in winter.

Irish people

About four million people live in Ireland. Today Ireland is a blend of the cultures of the many different peoples who have settled there over thousands of years.

A group of people called the Celts came to Ireland more than 2,000 years ago. Celtic laws, customs and their language live on. Irish comes from the language of the Celts.

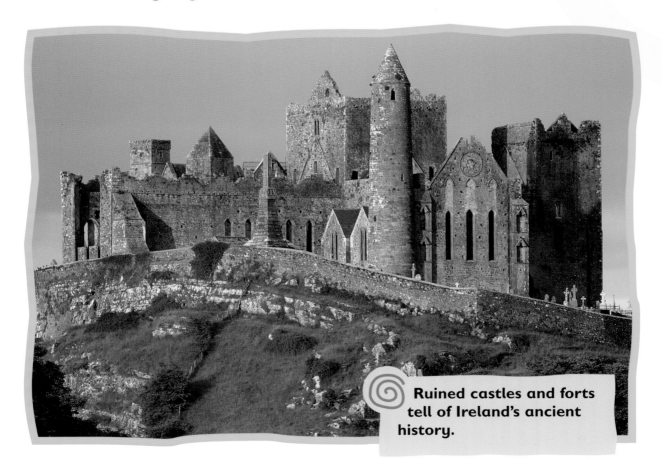

Ruined castles and forts tell of Ireland's ancient history.

Some road signs use both Irish and English, the two main languages of Ireland.

Did you know?

The feast day of Saint Patrick, the patron saint of Ireland, is a national holiday. Saint Patrick brought Christianity to Ireland in 432 CE.

People line the streets to watch the Saint Patrick's Day parade in Dublin.

Most people in the Republic of Ireland are Roman Catholics. Many of the rest belong to Protestant churches. Disagreements between Protestants and Catholics in Ireland and Northern Ireland caused fighting, unrest and violence for many years.

School and family

Irish children must go to school between the ages of six and sixteen but many start at nursery from the age of four.

Primary school is for students up to the age of twelve. Children study maths, reading, writing, computers, religion and Irish history and culture. Classes are taught in English, but children also learn Irish. Some schools teach all subjects in Irish. After school, children play sports, such as tennis and football, or take dance or music lessons.

Many children in Ireland go to schools run by the Catholic Church. Religion is an important part of everyday life.

Rugby is a popular after-school activity for many children.

After primary school, students attend secondary school. Many go on to college, university or job training.

Young people often live at home until they marry. Families eat meals and go to church together. They also gather to celebrate birthdays and holidays.

Families celebrate holidays, such as Saint Patrick's Day, together.

Country

For hundreds of years, most Irish people lived and worked in the countryside. Today, far less people work in farming, but it is still an important industry.

Most farms in Ireland are small family-owned businesses. Potatoes, wheat, sugar beet and turnips are the main crops. Some farmers also raise sheep, horses and dairy and beef cattle.

Some people earn extra money by providing services for tourists.

A child helps to care for a lamb.

Traditional crafts, such as knitting lace (left), still survive in the Irish countryside.

Fishermen catch cod and other saltwater fish off Ireland's coasts.

Pubs, markets and shops line the streets of this village. Some villages are tiny, with just a few houses.

Near Ireland's coasts, lakes and rivers, many people make their living by fishing. They catch trout, salmon, cod and other types of fish.

Almost every Irish village has a church. Community life is often focused around the church.

Did you know?

In the 1840s, a disease killed most of the Irish potato plants. Almost a million people starved to death in the famine that followed. That time is called the Great Famine.

City

Today, more than half of the people in Ireland live in or near cities. Dublin is the capital and it is also the largest city in Ireland. More than a million people live there.

Dublin has modern buildings next to historic churches and houses. It is also home to Ireland's oldest university, Trinity College.

Did you know?

One of the oldest books in the world is the *Book of Kells*. It is kept at Trinity College in Dublin.

People flock to Dublin's many shops, theatres and businesses.

This bridge crosses the River Liffey in Dublin.

A ferry leaves the town of Castletown Bearhaven in the southwest for Bear Island.

The River Liffey flows through Dublin, which is Ireland's busiest port. The country's second-largest city, Cork, is a major port on the River Lee. Other important ports are Galway and Limerick.

In the cities, many people take buses or taxis to work. Airports, railways and roads connect Irish cities. People travel to Great Britain by ferry or by aeroplane.

Irish homes

Most houses in Ireland are built of brick or cement. Those materials stand up well to rain. A typical house has four to seven rooms.

In the centre of Dublin, some people live in elegant houses built 200 years ago. Others live in modern flats or in houses in the large suburbs that surround Dublin.

Did you know?

The cost of housing in Ireland has risen sharply because Ireland has so many successful businesses. Many young people struggle to buy their own home.

There are many terraced houses like these, especially in cities.

In the countryside, some people live in old, stone cottages with thatched roofs. Many people, however, knock down old houses and replace them with modern bungalows.

This old cottage, built from stone, has a thatched roof made from reeds and straw.

Many homes are built of stone, brick and cement. Those materials cope with Ireland's rainy weather.

Food

Today, people eat all sorts of foods in Ireland. Traditionally, Irish people ate a lot of meals made from locally produced vegetables and meat or fish. Many Irish people continue to enjoy this type of food, using simple ingredients cooked well.

When people eat out, they can visit pubs and restaurants or buy fish and chips or other takeaways.

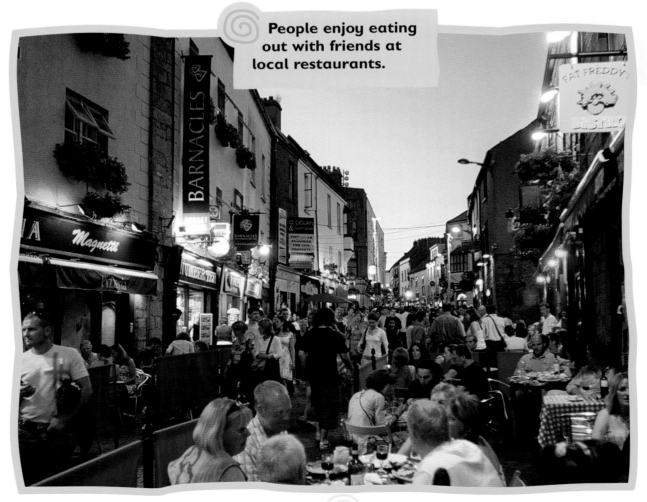

People enjoy eating out with friends at local restaurants.

Irish stew, made from lamb, potatoes and other vegetables, and soda bread make a tasty lunch.

Ireland is famous for its dairy products, beef and lamb. Irish people enjoy eating these foods and farmers sell a huge amount abroad. Near the coast, people also eat a lot of fish, shellfish and even seaweed. Potatoes are eaten with many meals. Colcannon, a famous Irish dish, is made from cooked potatoes, fried with onions, cabbage or leeks.

Did you know?

Soda bread is bread made with baking soda, rather than yeast, to make it rise. Irish people eat it with butter and jam, or with stews.

At work

Ireland has become a world leader in the making and selling of computers. Thousands of Irish people work in the computer industry. Other businesses are also doing well and employ many people. Then there are jobs in healthcare, government, education and tourism.

Did you know?

More than six million tourists visit Ireland each year.

World-famous crystal glass is made in the city of Waterford.

A worker puts together computers at a factory in Limerick.

A tourist guide tells visitors about Bunratty Castle and its past.

This farmer is using a wooden spade to cut peat.

Fishing, farming and mining are other important businesses. Many Irish food products are exported to other countries. Some people cut, dry and sell peat which is partly rotted plants. It is burnt as fuel and used in garden compost.

Having fun

Many people in Ireland enjoy watching and playing sport. Gaelic football is a very old sport that is still enjoyed today. It is a lot like football but players can touch the ball with their hands. Another popular sport is hurling which is like hockey but faster. Football is a favourite team sport, as is rugby.

People in Ireland also like to watch horse racing. The Irish Derby is a famous race held in County Kildare.

Each year, crowds of people watch the Irish Derby horse race.

Irish dancers wear colourful costumes and special shoes.

Birr Castle in Birr, central Ireland, has been a family home for more than 500 years. People can visit its gardens.

Traditional folk dancing and music are still popular in Ireland. The Irish also like going to the cinema, pubs, concerts and plays. Favourite outdoor activities include walking, biking, fishing, sailing and horse riding. Visiting Ireland's coasts and exploring its castles and forts are popular day trips.

Ireland: the facts

• English and Irish are the two languages of Ireland. English is used in everyday life.

• Ireland is a republic. Its president is the head of state. A prime minister handles the day-to-day running of the government.

• All of Ireland was once ruled by Great Britain. In 1921, Ireland was divided into two parts. Northern Ireland remained with Great Britain. (Great Britain and Northern Ireland are called the United Kingdom.) The southern part of Ireland became the Irish Free State. In 1949, it became the Republic of Ireland.

• People who are at least 18 years old may vote in the nation's elections.

• The flag of the Republic of Ireland has three bars. The green bar stands for the Roman Catholic people and the orange one for the Protestant people. The white bar is a symbol of hope for peace between the two groups.

The flag of Ireland has bars of green, white and orange.

• Ireland belongs to a group of countries called the European Union. Most of those countries, including Ireland, use the same currency, or money. It is called the euro. Euro paper money looks the same in all those nations. The fronts of euro coins also look the same, but the backs of the

The back of the Irish euro coin shows a harp. The harp is a symbol of Ireland.

coins are different. Each country has its own design. Irish euro coins have a picture of a harp, a symbol of Ireland's love for music.

The word shamrock comes from an Irish word that means 'little clover'.

Did you know?

The shamrock is a symbol of Ireland. This three-leaved clover is said to bring good luck.

Glossary

Bungalow a one-story house or cottage.

Counties regions or districts in a state or country.

Culture the traditions, way of living, beliefs and arts of nations or groups of people.

Emerald Isle a nickname for Ireland that comes from the green colour of the emerald gemstone.

Euro the currency, or money, used by many of the member nations of the European Union.

Export to sell and send goods to another country.

Famine a great shortage of food.

Ferries boats used to carry people, vehicles or goods across water.

Gaelic football an ancient sport in Ireland that is a lot like football, except that players are allowed to handle the ball.

Head of state the main representative of a country.

Hurling an ancient sport in Ireland that is similar to hockey but faster.

Peat bogs areas of wet, marshy land with partly rotted plant matter.

Port a town or city where ships take on or unload goods.

Pubs popular gathering places where people eat, drink and talk with family and friends.

Republic a kind of government in which decisions are made by the people of the country and their representatives.

Suburb an area of housing away from the city centre.

Thatched made of woven grass, straw or reeds.

Tourists people who travel to different places for fun.

Find out more

http://news.bbc.co.uk/cbbcnews/hi/guides/default.stm
Click on 'Northern Ireland' in the list of BBC Newsround guides for lots more information about Northern Ireland and Ireland.

www.irishpotatofamine.org/
An interactive site where you can learn all about the Irish potato famine.

Note to parents and teachers: Every effort has been made by the Publishers to ensure that these websites are suitable for children, that they are of the highest educational value, and that they contain no inappropriate or offensive material. However, because of the nature of the Internet, it is impossible to guarantee that the contents of these sites will not be altered. We strongly advise that Internet access is supervised by a responsible adult.

Some Irish words

You are more likely to hear English than Irish spoken in most of Ireland. However, in the west of the country you may hear some Irish. Here are a few Irish words and phrases.

English word	Irish word	Say...
hello	dia dhuit	djee-ah g-witch
goodbye	slan leat	slawn leat
cheers	sláinte	slawncha
please	le do thoile	leh duh hullay
water	uisce	ish-geh
food	bia	bee-yah
thank you	go raibh maith agat	guh row mah aguth
goodnight	oiche mháith	ee-heh wah

My map of Ireland

Trace this map, colour it in and use the map on page 5 to write the names of all the towns.

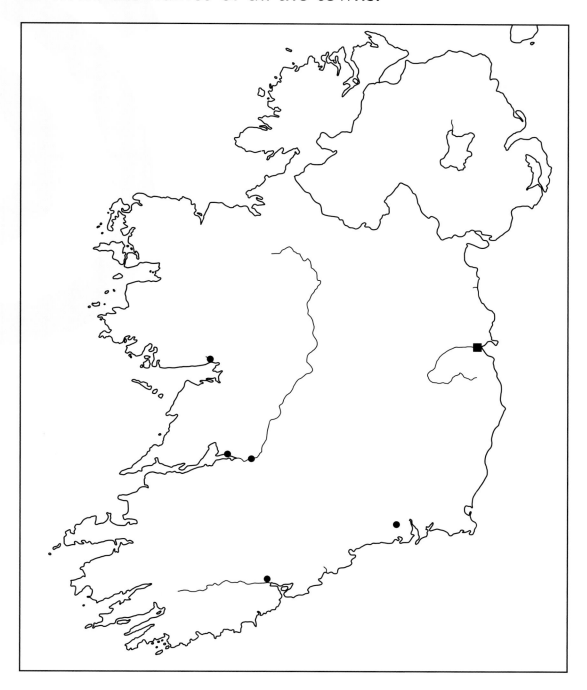

Index

Celts 10
cities 4, 5, 16–17, 18, 22
countryside 6, 9, 14–15, 19
currency 27, 28

dance 12, 25
Dublin 4, 5, 11, 16–17, 18

European Union 27, 28

families 13
famine 15
farming 6, 14–15, 21, 23
fishing 7, 15, 23, 25
flag 26
food 20–21

government 4, 5, 26
Great Britain 4, 5, 14, 17, 26

houses 18–19

industries 22–23

landscapes 6–7

languages 10, 11, 12, 26, 30

mining 23
mountains 6, 8
music 12, 25, 27

Northern Ireland 4, 11, 26

peat 6, 23, 28
population 10, 13
ports 17

religions 11, 12, 13, 15, 26

schools 12–13, 16
shamrock 27
sport 7, 12, 24–25, 28

tourism 14, 22, 23
transport 16–17

United Kingdom 4, 9, 26

weather 4, 7, 8–9, 19
work 14, 15, 22–23